IF

Greater Than a Tourist Book Series
Reviews from Readers

I think the series is wonderful and beneficial for tourists to get information before visiting the city.

-Seckin Zumbul, Izmir Turkey

I am a world traveler who has read many trip guides but this one really made a difference for me. I would call it a heartfelt creation of a local guide expert instead of just a guide.

-Susy, Isla Holbox, Mexico

New to the area like me, this is a must have!

-Joe, Bloomington, USA

This is a good series that gets down to it when looking for things to do at your destination without having to read a novel for just a few ideas.

-Rachel, Monterey, USA

Good information to have to plan my trip to this destination.

-Pennie Farrell, Mexico

Great ideas for a port day.

-Mary Martin USA

Aptly titled, you won't just be a tourist after reading this book. You'll be greater than a tourist!

-Alan Warner, Grand Rapids, USA

Even though I only have three days to spend in San Miguel in an upcoming visit, I will use the author's suggestions to guide some of my time there. An easy read - with chapters named to guide me in directions I want to go.

-Robert Catapano, USA

Great insights from a local perspective! Useful information and a very good value!

-Sarah, USA

This series provides an in-depth experience through the eyes of a local. Reading these series will help you to travel the city in with confidence and it'll make your journey a unique one.

-Andrew Teoh, Ipoh, Malaysia

>TOURIST

GREATER THAN A TOURIST- MÁLAGA SPAIN

50 Travel Tips from a Local

Zsuzsanna Udvarhelyi

Greater Than a Tourist- Málaga, Spain Copyright © 2019 by CZYK Publishing LLC. All Rights Reserved.

All rights reserved. No part of this book may be reproduced in any form or by any electronic or mechanical means including information storage and retrieval systems, without permission in writing from the author. The only exception is by a reviewer, who may quote short excerpts in a review.

The statements in this book are of the authors and may not be the views of CZYK Publishing or Greater Than a Tourist.

Cover designed by:
Cover Image:

CZYK Publishing Since 2011.

Greater Than a Tourist
Visit our website at www.GreaterThanaTourist.com

Lock Haven, PA
All rights reserved.

ISBN: 9781793129086

\>TOURIST

BOOK DESCRIPTION

Are you excited about planning your next trip?

Do you want to try something new?

Would you like some guidance from a local?

If you answered yes to any of these questions, then this Greater Than a Tourist book is for you.

Greater Than a Tourist- Málaga, Spain by Zsuzsanna Udvarhelyi offers some unique insider tips in Malaga and surroundings. Most travel books tell you how to travel like a tourist. Although there is nothing wrong with that, as part of the Greater Than a Tourist series, this book will give you travel tips from someone who has lived at your next travel destination.

In these pages, you will discover advice that will help you throughout your stay. This book will not tell you exact addresses or store hours but instead will give you excitement and knowledge from a local that you may not find in other smaller print travel books.

Travel like a local. Slow down, stay in one place, and get to know the people and the culture. By the time you finish this book, you will be eager and prepared to travel to your next destination.

>TOURIST

TABLE OF CONTENTS

BOOK DESCRIPTION
TABLE OF CONTENTS
DEDICATION
ABOUT THE AUTHOR
HOW TO USE THIS BOOK
FROM THE PUBLISHER
OUR STORY
WELCOME TO
> TOURIST
INTRODUCTION
1. Language Basics
2. How to order a coffee in Málaga and not die trying
3. Andalucía: The birthplace of Flamenco
4. Enjoy the sunset from one of my 'fantastic four'!
5. El Tintero de Málaga: the most interesting 'chiringuito' of the Costa del Sol
6. Experience the real local 'Tapeo' in the famous The Pimpi Florida, the tavern where everyone fits
7. Is it a rainy day? - Relax in the magical Hammam Al Andalus, the largest Arab baths in Spain.
8. Learn Salsa & Bachata while having a beer in Chiquita Cruz
9. Buy some fresh local produce in the Atarazanas Market

10. The city that never sleeps - Experience the Malagan Nightlife as a local!

11. Don't freak out when someone invites you for a drink in the middle of the street!

12. Getting there - Take the 'Cercanías' from the Airport

13. A route through the most interesting museums of Málaga

14. Go back in time! - La Alcazaba and Castillo de Gibralfaro places with a lot of History

15. Visit the one and only English Cemetery in Malaga - the oldest in the Iberian peninsula.

16. Discover the mysteries of the Passage of Chinitas!

17. Have a 'Churros with chocolate' for breakfast at Casa Aranda!.

18. Have a great tapas dinner in la Bodega El Pimpi and enjoy the views Roman Theater

19. Try the delicious 'Espetos de Sardinas' and the famous Boquerones!

20. Do the 'Siesta' as locals do!

21. If you don't follow the eating habit of Malaga you will stay hungry!

22. Try the famous fried salted almonds in the historic center.

23. Go for a walk and have a drink at La Malagueta

24. Stroll along the Paseo del Parque admiring its gardens, the Town Hall and the Bank of Spain.
25. Be part of the Great Filmfestival of Spain - Festival de Málaga
26. Enjoy a magical night with full of surprises and cultural activities - Noche en Blanco of Malaga
27. Watch a musical in the Cervantes Theater
28. Experience the Easter Holidays a little bit differently - Semana Santa of Malaga
29. Live the 'Feria of August' and drink the 'Cartojal' like the locals
30. Vivir una experiencia natural descendiendo el rio Chillar.
31. Good vibes only! - for Surf lovers
32. Enjoy the changing Sand Dunes at Playa Bolonia
33. Do nice trekking in Torcal de Antequera, a natural site of another planet
34. Enjoy the breathtaking views from the Balcony of Europa in Nerja
35. Spend a day in Puerto Banus, the most famous marina in Marbella
36. Seville, the city that fascinates the world
37. Cordoba, the city of three cultures
38. Granada, the Moorish jewel
39. Ronda, the dreaming city

40. Challenge your fear of heights in Caminito del Rey
41. Mijas, the town of the donkey-taxi
42. Los Alamos - beach party & kitesurf
43. Have a picnic at the Cave of the Cat
44. Setenil de las Bodegas
45. Parque Natural Sierra de Grazalema
46. Frigiliana, a white oasis
47. The pass of the Axarquía
48. Júzcar - the Blue village
49. Gibraltar, a country in a country
50. Talk to the people of Malaga and enjoy their company

TOP REASONS TO BOOK THIS TRIP

50 THINGS TO KNOW ABOUT PACKING LIGHT FOR TRAVEL

Packing and Planning Tips

Travel Questions

Travel Bucket List

NOTES

>TOURIST

DEDICATION

This book is dedicated to all the people who would love to explore this lovely region of Analucía. I promise you that once you arrive there you will fell in love. I will give some ideas that I as a local consider important because they reflect the feeling of Malaga

ABOUT THE AUTHOR

Zsuzsanna spent her University years in Málaga. During that time she was also working as a travel, events and nightlife advisor for international students organizing trips around Malaga region. She traveled around with locals and explored all the hidden places where the tourism still haven't put its footprint yet.

\>TOURIST

HOW TO USE THIS BOOK

The Greater Than a Tourist book series was written by someone who has lived in an area for over three months. The goal of this book is to help travelers either dream or experience different locations by providing opinions from a local. The author has made suggestions based on their own experiences. Please do your own research before traveling to the area in case the suggested places are unavailable.

Travel Advisories: As a first step in planning any trip abroad, check the Travel Advisories for your intended destination.
https://travel.state.gov/content/travel/en/traveladvisories/traveladvisories.html

FROM THE PUBLISHER

Traveling can be one of the most important parts of a person's life. The anticipation and memories that you have are some of the best. As a publisher of the Greater Than a Tourist book series, as well as the popular 50 Things to Know book series, we strive to help you learn about new places, spark your imagination, and inspire you. Wherever you are and whatever you do I wish you safe, fun, and inspiring travel.

Lisa Rusczyk Ed. D.
CZYK Publishing

OUR STORY

Traveling is a passion of the "Greater than a Tourist" series creator. Lisa studied abroad in college, and for their honeymoon Lisa and her husband toured Europe. During her travels to Malta, an older man tried to give her some advice based on his own experience living on the island since he was a young boy. She was not sure if she should talk to the stranger but was interested in his advice. When traveling to some places she was wary to talk to locals because she was afraid that they weren't being genuine. Through her travels, Lisa learned how much locals had to share with tourists. Lisa created the "Greater Than a Tourist" book series to help connect people with locals. A topic that locals are very passionate about sharing.

>TOURIST

WELCOME TO
> TOURIST

>TOURIST

INTRODUCTION

" I haven't been everywhere, but it's on my list. "
- Susan Sontag

Malaga is one of the eight Spanish provinces that make up the autonomous community of Andalusia. It is located to the south of the Iberian Peninsula, on the Mediterranean coast, between the provinces of Granada, to the east, and Cádiz, to the west. To the north, it borders the provinces of Córdoba and Seville. Its capital is the city of Málaga. The province is famous thanks to all its coastline, known worldwide as the Costa del Sol, which enjoys the privilege of being the third in terms of tourism in the Iberian Peninsula.

>TOURIST

1. LANGUAGE BASICS

Before you get lost in the narrow streets of the historic center and go for some shopping!

In the province of Malaga there are numerous shopping centers, markets, large stores and . and areas to make your most desired purchases, but honestly, the best you can do in order to make your shopping experience memorable is to dive into the historic center. You can find big and crowded shopping malls everywhere in the world, but Malaga has something unique that you won't find in all the places. You can start with the stunning Calle Larios where you will find fashion shops, boutiques, cafeterias, restaurants, perfumeries, jewelers, shoe shops ... But not only there are shops in Calle Larios since you can do 'shopping' in the historic center, so buying in Malaga will mean enjoying the city in all its senses. Close to Larios, there are other two streets I would recommend you as an expert of shopping. The first one would be Calle Nueva where you can find tons of local stores and the second and my favorite one would be Calle Granada which is totally exceptional in a way of its atmosphere during 365 days. That street is driving you from the Catedral till the Plaza de la Merced, which is also another really important spot for different reasons..(I know that you are really curious now, but will write about it later). You can continue your shopping route to the Port of Malaga, we call it 'Muelle Uno' or Pier One. It is an open shopping center next to the sea, where you can do all kinds of shopping, have ice cream, have lunch in one of its restaurants, or take a catamaran ride. All in the same place.

2. HOW TO ORDER A COFFEE IN MÁLAGA AND NOT DIE TRYING

Are you a lover of historic cafes and when visiting a city you always end up stopping along the way tasting a good cup of the best coffee? If this is the case and you are planning to visit Málaga, do not miss the emblematic Café Central, whose method of ordering coffee in Malaga has spread beyond the borders of the capital to cover practically the entire province. In effect, asking for a coffee goes to the non-local because it dominates a mathematical system of proportions that can confuse the most expert. Do not get discouraged because here we will explain how to order a coffee in Malaga and not die to try. Here is

>TOURIST

a short list that explains how coffee is served in Malaga: Solo (Black), largo (very strong), semi large (strong), mitad (half & half) semi corto (semi-short), corto (espresso), sombra (shade) or nube (cloud).

3. ANDALUCÍA: THE BIRTHPLACE OF FLAMENCO

One of the must-do things in Málaga is the Flamenco experience. There are several offers for Flamenco Shows in Málaga and during the years I lived there I saw all of them. The most authentic experience I had and probably the best one was in the Jardin restaurant which is located next to the gardens of the Málaga Cathedral, the Picasso Museum, the Roman Theater, and the Alcazaba. This building is one of the oldest one in town from the year 1887, offering the most exquisite selection of traditional Andalusian food mixed with incredible flamenco and tango shows. I like it especially because the place is owned by a local family and during the shows, you feel that you are part of the experience. Basically, the show is coming with a delicious and traditional dinner. During the high season you will be asked to book a full menu per person for a really reasonable price, and during the peak season normally you just have to in order to see the spectacular show.

4. ENJOY THE SUNSET FROM ONE OF MY 'FANTASTIC FOUR'!

In this section, you will get to know my favorite places for watching the sunset of Málaga. I have my own fantastic four. You might ask me why? Well, the reason is that there are four different places for different occasions or purposes. It depends on with who you are and how would you like to spend it. I would start with the Mirador de Gibralfaro which in my opinion is the best viewpoint of Malaga. You can go up with your friends or partner with a nice picnic bag and a good bottle of Rioja enjoying the stunning views of the city. If you would like to have a traditional sunset dinner at the beachfront I would recommend you to book a table at the restaurant El Balneario. Since its opening, at the edge of the twenties of the last century, until today, El Balneario has been at the top of the lists of favorite places of the locals. Contemplate the silhouette of the city in the background and the sun setting over the sea is one of the local pleasures par excellence. The gastronomic

>TOURIST

offer can be from the restaurant El Balneario (espetos, pescaíto, rice, fresh salads, and some meats), or more elaborate menus, always on request. Lastly, as we are living in the 'rooftops age' you cannot leave without having a great cocktail at one of the most 'cool' terraces in the center. There is no doubt that the Batik restaurant on the terrace of a nice hostel located on Alcazabilla street. Finally, I would say few terraces offer a view of Málaga in 360º. The privileged situation of the AC Málaga Palacio hotel makes it worthwhile to go for a drink simply to admire the city, it is El Ático, which is open all year round on the top floor. Furthermore, if you are a rooftop lover you can also check out the Terraza Club Chinitas and the Oasis Lounge.

5. EL TINTERO DE MÁLAGA: THE MOST INTERESTING 'CHIRINGUITO' OF THE COSTA DEL SOL

First of all, just to make it clear for your my lovely reader, chiringuito means 'beach restaurant or beach bar' in Spain. I am going to tell the story about one of the funniest moments of my experience in Malaga happened in the restaurant El Tintero. Of the many establishments that you can find on the coast, on El Palo beach, this is undoubtedly the most unique and famous. Keep reading and I'll explain the details. This restaurant is the only one where the dishes go to auction, although this is an explanation that falls short to describe what happens in this popular beach bar in Malaga. After sitting at a table a few meters from the sea and with a good umbrella, you will be given a drink note. From here you have to be attentive to all the waiters who are offering shouting some of the many dishes that they bring in an incredible balance with both hands. Keep your ears open to find out everything they offer, although they will see that they try to capture your attention in a very effective way. I love this restaurant and on every trip, I've made to Malaga I think I have not missed it once. You do not

>TOURIST

have to read several pages of the letter or listen to the role of a maître d 'recommending more dishes than you can remember exactly when it ends. No, here you have to let yourself be carried away by the impulse and fall into the temptation of what you see happening freshly prepared in front of you. It is what is called eating by sight. What do you have to do to order a dish? Something as easy as raising your hand and telling the waiter. You do not have to ask the price because it is the same for each dish that you eat.

6. EXPERIENCE THE REAL LOCAL 'TAPEO' IN THE FAMOUS THE PIMPI FLORIDA, THE TAVERN WHERE EVERYONE FITS

Pimpi Florida is a modest seafood restaurant in the El Palo neighborhood. Every local should go at least once in life, because opening the doors of Pimpi Florida is like activating the time machine, you immediately move to a very pleasant place, where you taste good seafood, you sing, you dance and you have a lot of fun, drinking white wine accompanied by peanuts and eating the famous dumplings that a neighbor brings each night and that is delicious, also shrimp pil-pil, clams, squid, carabineros, among many other things. This seafood restaurant with a tradition only opens at night, and to enter you have to keep a line because it is small inside. Closed on Mondays and Tuesdays.

7. IS IT A RAINY DAY? – RELAX IN THE MAGICAL HAMMAM AL ANDALUS, THE LARGEST ARAB BATHS IN SPAIN.

The truth is that Malaga is one of the sunniest places in Europe, but sometimes it can be a little bit cold and rainy, mostly in the winter time. The question is that: What should we do when it is rainy in Malaga? I have figured out the answer very quickly from one of my colleagues the first winter when It was an unusually rainy period. The Hammam Al Andalus in Malaga is an eccentric place, very well located near Calle Larios, exactly in the Plaza de Los Mártires, where once was the Medina of the city and next to the famous Carmen Thyssen Museum. When you arrive at the facilities, you begin to feel the vibration of a past, from the reception, where they attend you kindly, ready to help you from the first contact. Once ready, you go to enjoy the environments that feature this Nazari style enclosure, to let you wrap yourself in history, without clocks, without mobile, without anything more than the delivery to the relaxation and disconnection, although for a short time, they will be lavish moments. It is really amazing, even if it's a sunny day and you just want to relax a bit.

8. LEARN SALSA & BACHATA WHILE HAVING A BEER IN CHIQUITA CRUZ

One of my best experiences during my life in Malaga was learning salsa and bachata every Wednesday and Sunday in the bar called Chiquita Cruz in Plaza de Las Flores. It is a local bar with Caribbean vibes where you can enjoy live music, natural cocktails, free latin dance classes, pleasant attention, and a unique environment. The place itself is very tiny and when the classes are on, the whole bar is turning into a dancefloor.

9. BUY SOME FRESH LOCAL PRODUCE IN THE ATARAZANAS MARKET

Fruit, cheese, vegetables, meat, fish! The first hour of the day in the Atarazanas market, in Malaga, is typical of the rush hour on Wall Street. It is located one minute from the main arteries of the city: Alameda Principal and Calle Larios. Atarazanas is a place to see, buy, smell, touch ... and eat! It is one of the few markets that have several bars inside to enjoy a beer and a tapa between purchase and purchase. Honestly, this is the most beautiful market that I have ever seen in my life.

10. THE CITY THAT NEVER SLEEPS – EXPERIENCE THE MALAGAN NIGHTLIFE AS A LOCAL!

This part is very special for me because the Malagan Nightlife determined most of the time I lived there. As I was working as a travel, events and nightlife advisor, I was in touch with all the pubs and clubs in the city center. I also lived in Plaza de

>TOURIST

Mitjana which bars is another point to start the night. Hundreds of people gather in the square every weekend to take the first drinks of the night. If you wish something less crowded you can start in Plaza de la Merced which is also known for being the place where the famous painter, Picasso took his first steps, but apart from that, you can find plenty of bars offering pub crawls and discounts for the clubs. For the quilter looking for a drink and tranquility after dinner can go up to the terraces. As it was mentioned before, the AC Málaga Palacio hotel, Oasis Lounge, the terrace of the Molina Larios, Batik or Chinitas Lounge are some of them where you can enjoy a cocktail or a drink in a relaxed atmosphere. If you're looking for some commercial, EDM, reggaeton vibes you can go to Toulouse, Andén, Theatre, Malafama, Liceo or Sala Gold are the places where you'll find this musical style. My favorite one was Sala Gold, and not just because I used to work there. It's open from Monday to Sunday. They have Saxo and dance shows every night with a different style of music. Lovers of alternative music and locals who flee from the latest trends can visit El Muro, Drunkorama or Urbano. The Velvet, Metrica or ZZ Pub are the places where the march continues.

11. DON'T FREAK OUT WHEN SOMEONE INVITES YOU FOR A DRINK IN THE MIDDLE OF THE STREET!

If you are coming from another culture maybe it seems very weird for the first time that some stranger wants to invite you for a drink in the middle of the street. Don't worry! They don't want to hook up with you. They are professions associated with the world of the night or PR working for bars, pubs, and discotheques. They are the most attractive young people working on the streets convincing potential clients to visit their bar with exclusive promotions. For them then patience is the key to their success, no matter how many times they are rejected they will always keep - or do their best to do so - the smile throughout their workday. Neither the cold, nor the heat, nor having to spend the whole night standing undermine their will to make their party the most successful. You can accept a couple of cards and continue on your way to discovering the rest of the offers.

>TOURIST

12. GETTING THERE – TAKE THE 'CERCANÍAS' FROM THE AIRPORT

This is the fastest and cheapest or cheapest means of transportation to get from the Malaga airport to the center since the journey takes about 12 minutes while the Airport shuttle is more expensive and depending on the traffic, but more or less takes 30 minutes to get to the city center of Malaga. The distance is not as great as in other cities of the world, so if you travel a lot Malaga is the ideal city to stay. The first train leaves from Malaga airport to the center at 06.44 hrs and the last at 00.24 hrs. There is a frequency in every twenty (20) minutes.

13. A ROUTE THROUGH THE MOST INTERESTING MUSEUMS OF MÁLAGA

In the historic center of Malaga, we can visit the two main museums dedicated to the genius of Malaga: the Picasso Museum and the Picasso Birth House Museum. In addition, a few steps away, on Muelle Uno, you will find the Center Pompidou, where you can see works by Picasso and other artists. In the Picasso Museum, you can enjoy much of the artist's first works, as well as representative works throughout his career. The Casa Natal de Picasso Museum is located in the house of the Plaza de la Merced where Picasso was born and has sketches of such representative paintings as "Las señolas de Avignon", as well as personal memories, photographs and works by other artists of the time. The Center Pompidou of Malaga has a selection of 90 works by artists such as Picasso, Frida Kahlo, Antoni Tàpies and Orlan. It is one of my favorite museums because of its colorful cubic shape. You can also go to the Automobile Museum that has an exclusive collection of almost a hundred vehicles, as well as a collection of 200 pieces of Haute Couture from designers such as Channel, Dior, Paco Rabanne or Valentino. Without leaving the downtown area, we can visit the Carmen Thyssen Museum and the Contemporary Art Center (CAC Málaga).

>TOURIST

14. GO BACK IN TIME! – LA ALCAZABA AND CASTILLO DE GIBRALFARO PLACES WITH A LOT OF HISTORY

At the top of the city of Málaga, on Mount Gibralfaro, there are two places with a lot of history: La Alcazaba (which is a small version of the famous Alhambra of Granada) and the Castle of Gibralfaro. The Alcazaba is a fortress palace that was a property of the Muslim rulers of the city. It was built in the eleventh century on the slope of Mount Gibralfaro, on Roman ruins. Conceived with a totally military defensive mission, it consists of two walled enclosures accessed through multiple doors. At the top of the mountain, we find the Castle of Gibralfaro, which communicates with the Alcazaba through a walled ramp called La Coracha. As the locals told me the story, Castle of Gibralfaro was built in the 14th century with the aim of protecting the Alcazaba. Both of the places have spectacular views of the city, but if I have to choose, I would go for the Alcazaba because of its unique architecture and design. In my opinion, you can miss the visit to the Castle, but you should definitely go up to the Mirador del Gibralfaro which was mentioned in section 4.

15. VISIT THE ONE AND ONLY ENGLISH CEMETERY IN MALAGA – THE OLDEST IN THE IBERIAN PENINSULA.

The cemetery was built in 1831, and this is the oldest cemetery of the peninsula for non-Catholic Christians. Keep in mind that at that time the Protestant foreigners were not very well seen by the city, and by not allowing the burial of non-Catholics in normal cemeteries, the burials came to be done at nightfall, usually on little-crowded beaches. I remember when I started to climb the steep roads of the cemetery and I was already impressed by the first vision. They make guided tours in English and Spanish as well as night tours where they detail anecdotes and peculiarities of the cemetery, including Halloween night. A night visit is a really cool experience in my personal opinion. You should definitely do it if you have the chance! I think that a special place like that with 180 years of history cannot be forgotten because it has huge importance for the local community.

>TOURIST

16. DISCOVER THE MYSTERIES OF THE PASSAGE OF CHINITAS!

The Pasaje de Chinitas is one of those mythical corners of Málaga where history has special weight. This small pedestrian road was more than a key to the commercial and cultural growth of Malaga, and it was the meeting point of the main artistic figures of the country. The main reason? The creation of what was the legendary and well-known Café Chinitas, a place where you could enjoy plays and small concerts and had Federico García Lorca himself as a regular client. In addition to the Plaza de la Constitución -a wide and really beautiful building dating back to the 15th century- from the Chinitas Passage, you can access other areas of the city such as Calle Larios, the main commercial area of Málaga.

17. HAVE A 'CHURROS WITH CHOCOLATE' FOR BREAKFAST AT CASA ARANDA!.

Casa Aranda is perhaps the most well-known and visited breakfast place and 'churrería' (place dedicated to selling 'churros', one of the most typical breakfast in Spain) in Malaga, it may be due to its magnificent location, but I would say that is because of its more than 75 years of history. Through its streets pass daily a crowd of curious people from all over the world, with the clear intention of trying those delicacies that make this narrow street a truly unique and must-see site. I can be honest with you and trust me, that is probably the best churros I have ever had in my life during the time I lived in Spain.

\>TOURIST

18. HAVE A GREAT TAPAS DINNER IN LA BODEGA EL PIMPI AND ENJOY THE VIEWS ROMAN THEATER

Founded in 1971, El Pimpi is located in an old mansion in the 18th century and is one of the most traditional wineries in Málaga, where it is possible to enjoy local cuisine and local wines, but above all, the tradition and culture of the south of Spain. Through our halls have passed generations of personalities from the world of flamenco, politics, and art. It was not just my favorite restaurant in town. Antonio Banderas, the famous actor born in Malaga, bought the restaurant in 2017. The quality of the food is incredible and the prices are very reasonable in comparison to other restaurants in the city center.The visitor will be surprised by a hundred-year-old decoration that leaves no one indifferent, as well as a privileged environment surrounded by some of the most important historical monuments and cultural sites of our city: Alcazaba, Roman Theater, Picasso Museum, and the Plaza de la Merced.

19. TRY THE DELICIOUS 'ESPETOS DE SARDINAS' AND THE FAMOUS BOQUERONES!

Try the delicious espetos de sardinas (grilled sardines impaled on a cane), which are unique to Málaga and a hallmark of identity as well as ways to serve coffee in Malaga In the area of the beaches of El Palo, you can have freshly grilled sardine skewers for a ridiculously cheap price. Also 'Los boquerones al limón' or anchovies with lemon is one of the typical Malaga dishes that locals enjoy in 'chiringuitos' or beach bars. The interesting thing what few know that locals call themselves 'boquerones'. Why? Well, precisely, if something distinguishes this Andalusian city are the anchovies, which have become one of its biggest claims and one of its most recognized signs of identity. Therefore, the passage of time was forming the nickname of the people of Malaga related to one of their gastronomic identity. It was inevitable that in the end, the people of Malaga would end up adopting the nickname of 'boquerones'.

>TOURIST

20. DO THE 'SIESTA' AS LOCALS DO!

Most people know the Spanish lunch break as 'Siesta'. Especially in the southern territory in Spain, people love to do siesta which usually lasts from 2 pm till 5 pm, so you will find many shops and businesses closed during this time. Most local people travel home during the hottest hours of the day to enjoy a big lunch in their cool homes. Others go to tapas bars to eat together. If you are in Malaga I would definitely recommend you to follow this nice habit. Trust me, you will enjoy it!

21. IF YOU DON'T FOLLOW THE EATING HABIT OF MALAGA YOU WILL STAY HUNGRY!

Apart from the joke, it is really important. I remember when I moved to Malaga and it was
a huge struggle for me getting used to the Andalusian eating habits. They normally eat four times a day, sometimes five, which is totally fine, although these are not all "complete meals" according to the standard. The first typical meal of the day is

around 9 AM. Then the 'almuerzo', perhaps this could be Spanish brunch, it is usually eaten between 10:30 and 11:30, and the third meal of the day is technically what we call lunch around 2 PM or later. The fourth Spanish meal of the day is a snack. This meal could be considered basically as tea time around 5 PM. Finally, the last meal of the day arrives around 9 PM. or even later. There are different types of dinners but the most popular is to share some small tapas.

22. TRY THE FAMOUS FRIED SALTED ALMONDS IN THE HISTORIC CENTER.

The almond is the main dry fruit grown in the province of Malaga, where its crop now covers more than 16,000 hectares with productions that haul each season of 4,000 tons. You can find more and more local almond vendors in Malaga, but there is one very famous and where you find one of the best almonds. I can not imagine the corner of the Plaza de la Constitución without Pepe, the one with the almonds. I suppose that sometime when he retires, the government will have to make a statue for him. Apart from the joke, you can buy almond from all the

>TOURIST

vendors, and not only from Pepe. I just had to mention him, because he is basically a legend in Malaga.

23. GO FOR A WALK AND HAVE A DRINK AT LA MALAGUETA

This promenade is located in the neighborhood of La Malagueta and runs parallel to the Paseo Marítimo, The pedestrian walk known as Paseo Matías Prats, is the true seafront as such and is next to the beach of La Malagueta; with its 500 meters long it is full of cactus and palm trees. Once you reach the end of the walk, it changes its name to Paseo de La Farola, the name of the lighthouse symbol of the city and that was built in 1817. In the area, you can enjoy a good meal or drink overlooking the sea. At the beach, you will find plenty of nomad vendors trying to sell you a massage, beach towels or drinks. Is not that annoying like in Barcelona for example but if you feel that they would really bother you, just walk a little bit further from the touristy area.

24. STROLL ALONG THE PASEO DEL PARQUE ADMIRING ITS GARDENS, THE TOWN HALL AND THE BANK OF SPAIN.

Alameda Park or Paseo del Parque is a small oasis of 300 species of subtropical and tropical flora, which is a perfect place to take a deep breath of the fresh air during the hot summer days. In addition to the exuberant vegetation, the park has different busts, obelisks, fountains and monuments of illustrious figures such as Rubén Darío and Salvador Rueda. You can also find the buildings of the Town Hall, the Bank of Spain and the Directory of the University of Malaga. As I was living in the city center when I wanted to go to the beach I always started to walk from Calle Granada, Teatro Romano then down to the Paseo del Parque. It is a really nice walk to the Muelle Uno or to the Malagueta. From the Paseo, you have also access to the stairs of the Mirador del Gibralfaro (viewpoint mentioned before).

>TOURIST

25. BE PART OF THE GREAT FILMFESTIVAL OF SPAIN – FESTIVAL DE MÁLAGA

Festival de Málaga was born in 1998 and in each of its editions, it has aimed to achieve a series of objectives, including promoting the dissemination and promotion of Spanish cinematography, becoming a national and international reference in the field of cinematographic events and contribute to the development of Malaga as an open and cultural city. The festival projects the most important releases of the year of Spanish cinema, including documentaries and short films. It also awards prizes to the best films of the year as well as honorary awards. The main award is the Golden Biznaga for Best Film. Other winners, such as the Critics Award or Best Direction, receive Silver Biznagas. The festival also hosts roundtables and colloquiums on current issues for Spanish cinema. For ten days, the city will turn to the event: from the Teatro Cervantes, the festival's main stage, to the Albéniz cinema, through the Echegaray Theater, the magic of cinema will take over every corner, opening a new world before the eyes of the audience. Also in the streets of the city, you will breathe the atmosphere of the festival, with the coming famous guests who will enjoy the hectic cultural life and atmosphere of the bars, terraces, and restaurants of the historic center like the rest of the locals,

26. ENJOY A MAGICAL NIGHT WITH FULL OF SURPRISES AND CULTURAL ACTIVITIES – NOCHE EN BLANCO OF MALAGA

The Noche en Blanco or 'White Night' in English consists of a total of 204 activities in up to 112 spaces. The program is divided into different categories such as Art, Museums and Exhibitions, Artistic Actions in the street, Music and dance, visits and extraordinary activities. You can check the official website of the Noche en Blanco de Málaga so you do not miss any of the activities. This is one of my favorite event in Malaga because you can find tons of surprises and activities on the streets. If you want to experience some cultural and traditional activities surrounded by a fun environment, make sure that you check the dates before you travel to Malaga.

>TOURIST

27. WATCH A MUSICAL IN THE CERVANTES THEATER

The Cervantes Theater of the Spanish city of Malaga is one of the oldest scenic spaces of the capital of the Costa del Sol, dates from 1870 and has one thousand two hundred seats. If you are a Broadway musical or just a simple theater lover, I would really recommend you to check out the event calendar and book a ticket during your stay. I had the chance to see the Chicago and Dirty Dancing there and it was an unforgettable experience even if it was my first year in Malaga and I did not understand anything in Spanish, but as they are so incredibly professionals you can understand the whole story just by watching it.

28. EXPERIENCE THE EASTER HOLIDAYS A LITTLE BIT DIFFERENTLY – SEMANA SANTA OF MALAGA

The Semana Santa or 'Holy Week' is the period that begins with Palm Sunday and ends with Easter Sunday. During these 8 days, the streets of the historic center of Malaga will be closed to traffic because they are visited by certain people from Malaga and tourists from all over the world who want to be part of the many processions that leave every day. I have several tips for you as I lived that events several times and it is better that you prepare for it before you go. Although this advice may surprise you, it is not always a good thing to book an accommodation in the city center during the Holy Week. The processions are so many in the city, that sometimes you can see yourself locked in the streets without exits until the early hours of the morning. It depends on what your plans are, you have to consider how and when you will want to arrive at your accommodation to rest, since if you do not plan this before you can see yourself in some logistics problem to reach your accommodation. The other important fact that you should know that the prices of accommodation and restaurants in the city of Malaga may be affected by a significant increase. Book the accommodation well in advance and ask for restaurant menus before you sit down. My third tip would be to find out about the schedules and routes of the "brotherhoods". To enjoy the processions and see the entire route of each one, it is best to know the times and routes of the Thrones. Printed guides are

\>TOURIST

distributed by tourist establishments that you can obtain without difficulty and there are also mobile applications such as the "Semana Santa Málaga" app that will be of great help to you. Last but not least, during these 8 days, the city of Malaga is totally blocked by this religious and spectacular event. Crossing a street could be a very complicated action that takes a long time and the only thing you can do is: arm yourself with patience!

29. LIVE THE 'FERIA OF AUGUST' AND DRINK THE 'CARTOJAL' LIKE THE LOCALS

The Malaga fair is held every August. It may not be as well known as the April fair in Seville, but I can promise you that it is the same or more fun and that it is worth coming to live it. In fact, the first time I visited Malaga, it was during the fair and since then it is still one of my favorite celebrations. If you trust me I give you a list of my best tips to enjoy the fair as local. The first day normally on a Friday there is fireworks on the beach at midnight. Then Saturday morning is the perfect opportunity to go to the center to see the Romería where there is a parade of horses and people singing from their carts through the historic center. Good to know that The Malaga Fair is divided into two parts: the fair in the streets of the historic center and the Real one. The Real is where you will find the attractions of the fair, the booths, and the Andalusian atmosphere. Going to the Real one during the day is seeing the most traditional part of the fair. I advise you to go to eat and then have a drink and enjoy the music until the sun begins to fall. I also used to enjoy the downtown fair, but it is true that in recent years it has become more and more chaotic. What used to be a way to bring the atmosphere of the fair to the center, has become a street party that is sometimes too uncontrolled and with little relation to an Andalusian fair. Most of the locals are dressed up in a traditional flamenco costume, singing and drinking the most typical drink of the fair which is a sweet white wine with the fuchsia label called Cartojal and the Rebujito (chamomile with sprite). Is it easy to find accommodation in Malaga during the Fair week?

Being sincere NO. If you plan to come to the Feria de Málaga, it is better to go ahead of time and look for accommodation with time. Because it is a festival where the city receives lots of visitors, we must add

>TOURIST

that it is summer, it is a coastal city and one of the top tourist destinations throughout the year.

30. VIVIR UNA EXPERIENCIA NATURAL DESCENDIENDO EL RIO CHILLAR.

This hike through the river was the most refreshing and fun experience I had in Malaga. This aquatic route, called Río Chillar you can do perfectly with children since it is not necessary to do it whole, you can turn around when you want if you see that the road gets difficult or they are tired. Most of the route is made by the river bed, so you will be wet most of the time. The water in very few parts covers and it is not necessary to know how to swim to do the entire hike. Yes, there are large pools where you can swim and take a dip, but I insist that it is a perfect route for all ages. The river Chillar is located between the municipalities of Nerja and Competa (Málaga), in the easternmost part of the province in the middle of the natural park of the Sierras de Almijara and Alhama. Arriving at the river is easy, although if you do not walk with your eyes wide open, you may pass it by. The place is accessible by car. You have to take the

N-340 towards Almería, then cross the Chillar river bridge, continue along the avenue until the third roundabout where you take Julio Romero street, later on, Avenida de la Constitución. After 3 kilometers you take the Camino de Los Almanchares where the asphalt road disappears and leads to another gravel road. Ready! We have already arrived. Do not worry if at first, you do not see water, it happens to many people who are surprised and disappointed to start the route and see everything dry, these are only the first meters. The first thing you will see is a light factory and this is where the fun begins. Along the route, you will find areas with strong waterfalls, quieter and deeper areas where you can swim and others just for a walk. There's no more.

31. GOOD VIBES ONLY! – FOR SURF LOVERS

In Malaga, you will not find waves of world quality but when they work they are very fun and allow you to perform all kinds of maneuvers that will make you finish your surfing day very satisfied. In this section, I will share the two of my favorite surf spots close to Malaga. Even if you are not a surfer,

>TOURIST

you can just do a day trip there, since those beaches are breathtaking. Just a couple hours from Malaga where the Atlantic Ocean and the Mediterranean Sea meet each other there is the beach called Los Lances in Tarifa, a unique place to practice surfing. Just 14 kilometers from Africa, this piece of coastline is built, which is the continuous pilgrimage of surfers from all over the world. The strong wind that blows in the area causes high waves to be able to develop all kinds of acrobatics. If you are passionate about surfing, specially kite-surfing and at the same time enjoy a good landscape, do not hesitate and go to Tarifa. Close to Tarifa, my favorite surf beach is El Palmar. This beach located in Vejer de la Frontera has waves of almost three meters and is the meeting place of the largest number of surfers in Spain. In fact, it appears in all the lists of the best beaches in Spain to practice this sport. If you like this environment and want to enjoy surfing do not hesitate and go to El Palmar. In addition, the surf culture is rooted in the population and many bars and shops have specialized in this sport.

32. ENJOY THE CHANGING SAND DUNES AT PLAYA BOLONIA

I think the Playa Bolonia is one of the most beautiful and wild beaches in Spain. The Playa de Bolonia is an almost wild beach located in the municipality of Tarifa, about 2 hours by car from Malaga town. Bolonia is more than a beach, it is a natural environment with places full of almost virgin nature, fine white sand, crystal clear waters, and a pleasant sea breeze. It is a very clean beach and its waters are the most transparent in the area. Those who visit it understand that it is a unique natural environment and respect it. I remember when I was there I had a lot of fun sliding down from its impressive sand dunes. Take a day trip there if you are traveling during the summer season!

>TOURIST

33. DO NICE TREKKING IN TORCAL DE ANTEQUERA, A NATURAL SITE OF ANOTHER PLANET

The Torcal de Antequera is a spectacular stone formation sculpted by wind and water over millions of years. A natural wonder in Malaga that you should not miss. This beautiful Karstic landscape is located between the towns of Antequera and Villanueva de la Concepción about 1-hour drive from Malaga center. With its columns, caves and limestone discs, it is a magical place, very different from any other site you have seen so far. It is worth taking a walk along its paths, where in addition to strangely shaped stones you can see eagles, vultures, mountain goats, and other animals. Take good trekking shoes with you and also some warm clothes, because even in summer it can be really cold up there.

34. ENJOY THE BREATHTAKING VIEWS FROM THE BALCONY OF EUROPA IN NERJA

For me, the Balón de Europa in Nerja or 'The Balcony of Europe' is undoubtedly one of the most emblematic places in Spain. An icon that nobody wants to miss when visiting this beautiful town in the province of Malaga. This incredible viewpoint located in the center of Nerja. One of the most famous places in Andalusia. An idyllic place to take a panoramic photo of the Mediterranean Sea or to pose next to the famous statue of King Alfonso XII. Rey, who baptized this wonderful place in his visit to Nerja after the earthquake that occurred in the year 1884. The fact that occurred when he peeked out at what was formerly a point of surveillance for the enemies, called Paseo de la Batería and shouted "this It's the Balcony of Europe. " From the balcony, through the stairs, you can access to a small beach, and if you continue to explore you will find hidden lagoons with some natural caves.

>TOURIST

35. SPEND A DAY IN PUERTO BANUS, THE MOST FAMOUS MARINA IN MARBELLA

A day in Puerto Banús is one of the activities that you have to do during your stay in Malaga, to also know the glamorous facet of the province. The first thing that people usually visit are the docks, here there are yachts and boats of all kinds, and very often you can see Maserati, Ferrari or Lamborghini cars parked there. Along the Paseo del Muelle Ribera the restaurants follow each other, alternating with fashion boutiques of the best global brands. Walking here is a pleasure, although there are always many people. If you come at night, right in the first street parallel to the pier there are many bars and pubs to have a drink, before continuing the nightclub party. The beaches extend both to the right and to the left of the Puerto Deportivo, you can enjoy the sun and take a bath to escape the heat, or decide to stop visiting Puerto Banús and spend the day at a beach club. If the day is not hot, you can also take a long walk from Puerto Banús to Marbella following the promenade, leaving luxury villas and mansions aside, and on the other the beach and the sea. The walk is beautiful and the views are unique, but if you decide to do it, keep in mind that you will have to walk for a couple of hours to get to Marbella.

36. SEVILLE, THE CITY THAT FASCINATES THE WORLD

If you have time for a day trip, then make sure that you don't miss Seville. The city has it all. There you will be able to witness history, while you will be part of a modern city that evolves under a human and sustainable model. An amazing city that encourages you to enjoy culture, gastronomy, leisure, and sports. Located on the banks of the Guadalquivir River, Seville is the heir to a rich Arab legacy and its status as a prosperous commercial port with the Americas. The Andalusian capital exudes joy and bustle in each of the streets and squares that make up its historic center, which houses an interesting set of buildings declared World Heritage and neighborhoods of deep popular flavor, such as Triana or La Macarena. All this without forgetting the numerous terraces, bars, and bars where you can practice one of the most ingrained and tasty customs of the city: the "tapas". Another good excuse to get closer to the capital of Seville are its parties. Declared of International

>TOURIST

Tourist Interest, Holy Week and the April Fair reflect the devotion and folklore of the Sevillian people, always open and cordial with the visitor. If you are planning to go to Seville make sure that you visit the Plaza de España which is apart from the fact that it's beautiful, you have to know that some parts of the famous Star Wars and also Games of Thrones was filmed there.

37. CORDOBA, THE CITY OF THREE CULTURES

Córdoba is one of those great Spanish cities of an inescapable visit. With an impressive cultural background, Córdoba has been a Roman and Muslim capital and has been the cradle of universal characters such as Séneca, Averroes or Maimónides. The old town of Córdoba has enough charms to keep a tourist busy for at least one day. The point of reference is the Mosque-Cathedral. Around it is woven the tangle of narrow streets that make up the charming center of the city, and that along with the river and its Roman bridge, form a picture of great beauty and charm. If you travel to Malaga for more than a week, you should not miss the opportunity to know Córdoba.

38. GRANADA, THE MOORISH JEWEL

My other day trip tip would be Granada which is truly one of the jewels of Spain and one of the most visited places by tourists from all over the world. What was for so long the capital of Al Andalus, or Moorish Andalusia, offers us some of the most important memories of this historic Spanish era, with the world-famous Alhambra at the head of the list. You will walk through dream gardens, charming narrow streets full of flowers or sit in one of those typical taverns to try the famous Trévelez ham with local wine. Here you can breathe so many centuries of history that will surround you wherever you are. At the mount of Sacromonte, you can attend some gypsy flamenco shows in the caves. In these famous caves of Sacromonte gypsies lived for centuries, and still do some, making a magnificent craft. Also "Sierra Nevada" (whose peak, the Mulhacen, with its 3,478 meters of height, is the highest in the Iberian Peninsula) offers excellent conditions for winter sports; On the other hand, it is very close to the Mediterranean coast, which makes it the ideal place to visit at any time of the year.

>TOURIST

39. RONDA, THE DREAMING CITY

Ronda is located in the heart of the Serrania de Ronda, about 100 km from the city of Malaga and with a population of approximately 35,000 inhabitants. Surrounded by lush river valleys and sitting on a deep gully, Ronda is a paradise worth visiting. Anyone who has been lucky enough to visit Ronda, like I understand its appeal. It is one of the most beautiful and visited cities in Spain (the third most visited city in Andalusia). Ronda is simply spectacular. It was the most beloved city of Andalusia by Ernest Hemingway, who wrote of it in several of his works. He also fell in love with Orson Welles, whose ashes lie in the city. Would it be for something, right? The most striking feature of Ronda is its nearly 100-meter high bridge over the Tagus River linking the two parts of the city. You can not miss the old town or the wine fountains!

40. CHALLENGE YOUR FEAR OF HEIGHTS IN CAMINITO DEL REY

The Caminito del Rey or 'The little path of the King' is a passage built on the walls of the Los Gaitanes gorge, next to the village of El Chorro, which serves as a boundary between the municipalities of Ardales, Álora, and Antequera, in the province of Málaga. It is a pedestrian walkway of more than 3 kilometers, attached to the rock inside a canyon, with sections of a width of just 1 meter, hanging up to 100 meters above the river, in almost vertical walls. It is important that before you buy your ticket, plan your visit and carefully read the rules of mandatory use. I am a nature lover, so for me, this excursion would be the most. You get there easily but public transportation, but I would recommend you to rent a car because on the way you will want to stop every 5 minutes to photograph something. Believe me, you cannot miss it!

>TOURIST

41. MIJAS, THE TOWN OF THE DONKEY-TAXI

The beautiful picture of endless white houses ascending the slopes of the Sierra de Mijas contrasts with the intense green of the pines offering one of the most recognizable and picturesque images of Andalusia. The town is formed by three urban centers that are; Mijas Pueblo, located at the foot of the homonymous mountain at 430 m above sea level, Las Lagunas is the most modern part of the municipality, linked to Fuengirola, and La Cala located on the shores of the sea with more than 12 km of coastline where the municipality offers a large number of beaches for all tastes. Mijas is a tiny town on the Cuesta del Sol, half an hour from Malaga. The typical Andalusian streets of white houses and pots with geraniums. Also in Mijas, they have donkey-taxis or in Spanish, 'burro-taxis'. I know you don't have a clue what I'm talking about. I am going to explain to you. During the sixties, there were workers who used the donkey as a means of transport and often the tourists wanted to go for a walk or take pictures with them. This is how the burro-taxi was born, which nowadays make tourist routes.

42. LOS ALAMOS – BEACH PARTY & KITESURF

Los Álamos beach, in Torremolinos, is located between the Playamar beach and the limit with the municipality of Málaga. Possibly one of the most lively beaches of the entire Costa del Sol thanks to its huge leisure offer. If you take the 'Cercanías' train from Malaga center you can get there in 15 minutes. The beach of Los Alamos is perfect to enjoy the summer days for its many activities, it is ideal for kitesurfing, as well as relax in one of the pubs chill outs that are there. Do you come with small children? The pedal boats are the best activity to do as a family. If this has seemed a little you can also enjoy water bikes, banana, jet boat. Everything you imagine gathered on the same beach. But the animation of this beach does not end here and neither when the sun sets because the high offer of beach clubs will make you enjoy the night in the best atmosphere. Finally, note that in July is celebrated Los Alamos Beach Fest, a festival of music and shows on the beach, claim for all lovers of electronic music.

>TOURIST

43. HAVE A PICNIC AT THE CAVE OF THE CAT

The 'Cueva del Gato' or in English the Cave of the Cat in Ronda is one of those paradisiacal fluvial pools that are usually found throughout the Andalusian geography. But unlike many others, access to Cueva del Gato is very simple, since you can park just a few meters away. It is for this access so comfortable that the Cueva del Gato is usually quite busy during the summer months, especially on weekends. The water is crystal clear, very clean and exceptionally cold. It is a fantastic place to go on a picnic and cool off after a morning of sightseeing. The Cueva del Gato is one of the most unique cave complexes in Andalusia. It has two entrances, one to the north in Hundidero and the other to the south in the Cueva del Gato. The name of this cave comes from its supposed feline appearance since it is said that the mouth of the cave looks like the face of a cat. If you are coming from Ronda follow the signs in the direction of Seville. After about 5 km, you will see a sign for Benaoján / Monteque, turn left and follow that road. After approximately 6 km you will find a parking area on the right as in the photograph.

44. SETENIL DE LAS BODEGAS

Setenil de las Bodegas is a beautiful town of Cádiz, known especially for the particularity of its homes. These, in addition to being excavated in the mountain, have their whitewashed facades, so the municipality is part of the famous Route of the White Villages. If you want to know more about this peculiar locality, do not hesitate to continue reading. Actually, I found this place accidentally by driving through Ronda and I had to stop because it was spectacular. I haven't seen a natural wonder like this before. The municipality is declared a Historic-Artistic Site due to the beauty and originality of its urban structure. And it is that its streets are adapted to the course of the Guadalporcún river, a reason why we can be with a type of house known like "shelter under rocks". These are outgoing and natural caves used as houses and where temperatures are always fresh in summer.

>TOURIST

45. PARQUE NATURAL SIERRA DE GRAZALEMA

The Sierra de Grazalema is located between the Andalusian provinces of Cádiz and Málaga and it is one of the most spectacular karst complexes in Spain, with deep gorges, chasms and the most extensive set of rivers, cavities and underground galleries in Andalusia. The entire territory of the Sierra de Grazalema Natural Park was declared a Biosphere Reserve by Unesco in 1977. The Sierra de Grazalema rises in front of the ocean, like a gigantic wall. Its slopes are home to small white villages while slowing the storms that come from the Atlantic and make this mountain is the rainiest place in the Iberian Peninsula. If you want to enjoy the history, culture, and cuisine of Cádiz and rest a few days with your family, don't miss this place.

46. FRIGILIANA, A WHITE OASIS

There is no list in the world about what places you should not miss in the province of Malaga that does not include this beautiful corner of Malaga. In fact, it is considered one of the most beautiful villages in Spain. Whitewashed streets, cobbled sidewalks, windows full of colorful flowers and an environment difficult to express with words. To understand the charm of Frigiliana well, you have to visit it. Spending a couple of hours in this paradise is well worth it. You can also visit the Archaeological Museum of the Axarquía -where the town is located-, try its famous cane honey or go to the Botanical Garden of Santa Fiora. Stroll through its streets, find the most beautiful places and enjoy the charm of this little corner of the province of Malaga. To end the experience, it will not hurt to climb up to El Fuerte hill, 963 meters high, and relax contemplating the beautiful views of the town.

>TOURIST

47. THE PASS OF THE AXARQUÍA

The Arabs already said that, precisely in the region of Malaga's Axarquía, what they considered the best raisin in the world was generated. Almánchar, Moline, Comares or Cútar are just some of the towns that make up the Ruta de la Pasa, an interesting tour that will take you to know the ancestral production system that continues to develop in this area of Malaga and, of course, we should Include in our proposals on what to do in Malaga. Also in the Axarquía, the famous muscatel sweet wine is elaborated in a traditional way, something that you should not miss in any of the family wineries scattered around the area. The curious orography of this area of Malaga, full of ridges and steep slopes, is used both for the extraction of the raisins and for the planting of vineyards. Another positive aspect is the weather conditions - the sun that shines so bright in this area of Malaga and the temperatures - ideal for producing this delicacy from Málaga.

48. JÚZCAR – THE BLUE VILLAGE

Júzcar is the municipality of the province of Malaga that since 2011 was renamed Smurf Village when it was chosen to promote the film of the famous cartoons. Their houses acquired the blue color of the popular characters created by the cartoonist 'Peyo'. This change of image caught the attention of the world and tourists and began to open bars and shops. However, a few years later the town was disowned and can no longer be called Smurf Village because of problems with copyright. People call daily to see if the town is still painted blue. We continue as we were, the characters stay on the street, follow the same infrastructure as before, the dolls, everything ... But now we have more activities. Now the 'Blue Village', is designed for families and especially for children and has zip lines, climbing a wall, Tibetan bridges, hiking trails and of murals, children's playground and a suspension route through footbridges. Close to the village, you will find plenty of hiking trails with beautiful views. The way up to the village is also breathtaking.

>TOURIST

49. GIBRALTAR, A COUNTRY IN A COUNTRY

One of the excursions that you can not stop doing if you are on vacation in Andalusia is to spend at least one day in Gibraltar, a small piece of land located in the southernmost part of the Iberian Peninsula that extends over the monolithic promontory of the Rock of Gibraltar. Because of its privileged strategic location -front between two continents (Europe and Africa) and two seas (Atlantic and Mediterranean).) - Gibraltar has been a disputed territory since antiquity, despite its small area of only 7 km2. The rock is, from 1713, a property of the crown of the United Kingdom, since its sovereignty was transferred to the kingdom of Great Britain by means of the Treaty of Utrecht after the war of Spanish Succession. Therefore, its official language is English, although practically all its inhabitants also speak Spanish (and also with a strong Andalusian accent!). Also on the border, there is a tourist information office where you can get a map of Gibraltar (bad enough, by the way). Keep in mind that it is not to scale, so even if on the map it seems that the distances are not too big, the whole area east of Main Street is in slope (towards the rock), and many of the streets are very steep or have endless stairs. My advice is to rent a car for this excursion, then you can drive up to the Rock and enjoy the spectacular views. If you are lucky, and the weather is clear you will see Africa from the top. It is also possible that you will get robbed by the monkeys while you are outside of the car. They are really tricky.

50. TALK TO THE PEOPLE OF MALAGA AND ENJOY THEIR COMPANY

My last tip would be very easy and simple. If you really want to have the local experience, just meet and talk to local people. This is the best way to spend your holidays properly.

>TOURIST

TOP REASONS TO BOOK THIS TRIP

Gastronomy: Most of the experts on the cuisine of Malaga agree in highlighting the simplicity of the ingredients used, the variety and richness of their dishes and their special flavor. All these characteristics are not more than the result of optimal use of the best natural products used in the elaboration of its extensive cookbook; a cookbook, by the way, that sticks perfectly to the Mediterranean diet, so accredited by its more than demonstrable health qualities.

Night Live: The nightlife in Málaga offers you the opportunity to explore the streets of the capital. Here you can find from traditional tapas bars to modern nightclubs. In the center of Málaga modern and classic combine to form the main leisure artery of the capital. The nearby streets are a maze of tapas bars and wine cellars where you can buy wine, including the typical Málaga sweet wine. In addition, on weekends, many young people come to the bars and pubs to enjoy the nightlife in Malaga. The people of

Malaga do not usually leave before 12 midnight and sometimes they do not return until dawn, of course ... not without having enjoyed a good breakfast along the way.

Quality of Life: Málaga has the highest quality of life surveys. In fact, it is among the top ten European cities that score. The Eurobarometer, which was carried out in 2015 in 79 EU locations, gathers the perception of European citizens about the quality of life in their populations, analyzing aspects such as the state of infrastructures, the feeling of security, environmental pollution, job opportunities or green spaces, among others.

Never boring: Malaga is the most nocturnal European city and the fourth in the world, far ahead of New York. The terraces and nightclubs open their doors until the early hours of the morning, offering a good dose of entertainment and entertainment. Hotel Larios and Málaga Palacio, for example, have terraces located in the attic, where outdoor parties are repeated night after night, with live performances of flamenco and jazz. But this nightlife does not stop

>TOURIST

there. All those who prefer to keep their feet on the ground, opt for the terraces of the Plaza del Obispo, for example, crowded with people any day of the week. People who take advantage of the hours of less heat, when the sun has set, to make life on the street. Away from the Center, at Playa de Los Alamos there is a row of beach bars that remain open from morning until late in the morning. They go from being restaurants or coffee shops to becoming authentic nightclubs. Perfect places for a good meal after a sunny morning and even better for a few drinks and dancing after dinner. These are just some of the many examples of activity, party, and fun that we can find in Malaga. What's more, the study carried out by the social network ensures that many pubs and clubs in Malaga open their doors after midnight and remain open until the sun rises. In addition, the people of Malaga are very willing to leave the premises with the first rays of light and make a stop for breakfast before going home. Therefore, it is not surprising that it has established itself as the most active city during the 24 hours.

>TOURIST

BONUS BOOK

50 THINGS TO KNOW ABOUT PACKING LIGHT FOR TRAVEL

PACK THE RIGHT WAY EVERY TIME

AUTHOR: MANIDIPA BHATTACHARYYA

First Published in 2015 by Dr. Lisa Rusczyk. Copyright 2015. All Rights Reserved. No part of this publication may be reproduced, including scanning and photocopying, or distributed in any form or by any means, electronic or mechanical, or stored in a database or retrieval system without prior written permission from the publisher.

Disclaimer: The publisher has put forth an effort in preparing and arranging this book. The information provided herein by the author is provided "as is". Use this information at your own risk. The publisher is not a licensed doctor. Consult your doctor before engaging in any medical activities. The publisher and author disclaim any liabilities for any loss of profit or commercial or personal damages resulting from the information contained in this book.

Edited by Melanie Howthorne

ABOUT THE AUTHOR

Manidipa Bhattacharyya is a creative writer and editor, with an education in English literature and Linguistics. After working in the IT industry for seven long years she decided to call it quits and follow her heart instead. Manidipa has been ghost writing, editing, proof reading and doing secondary research services for many story tellers and article writers for about three years. She stays in Kolkata, India with her husband and a busy two year old. In her own time Manidipa enjoys travelling, photography and writing flash fiction.

Manidipa believes in travelling light and never carries anything that she couldn't haul herself on a trip. However, travelling with her child changed the scenario. She seemed to carry the entire world with her for the baby on the first two trips. But good sense prevailed and she is again working her way to becoming a light traveler, this time with a kid.

>TOURIST

INTRODUCTION

*He who would travel happily
must travel light.*

-Antoine de Saint-Exupéry

Travel takes you to different places from seas and mountains to deserts and much more. In your travels you get to interact with different people and their cultures. You will, however, enjoy the sights and interact positively with these new people even more, if you are travelling light.

When you travel light your mind can be free from worry about your belongings. You do not have to spend precious vacation time waiting for your luggage to arrive after a long flight. There is be no chance of your bags going missing and the best part is that you need not pay a fee for checked baggage.

People who have mastered this art of packing light will root for you to take only one carry-on, wherever you go. However, many people can find it really hard to pack light. More so if you are travelling with children. Differentiating between "must have" and "just in case" items is the starting point. There will be ample shopping avenues at your destination which are just waiting to be explored.

This book will show you 'packing' in a new 'light' – pun intended – and help you to embrace light packing practices for all of your future travels.

Off to packing!

DEDICATION

I dedicate this book to all the travel buffs that I know, who have given me great insights into the contents of their backpacks.

THE RIGHT TRAVEL GEAR

1. CHOOSE YOUR TRAVEL GEAR CAREFULLY

While selecting your travel gear, pick items that are light weight, durable and most importantly, easy to carry. There are cases with wheels so you can drag them along – these are usually on the heavy side because of the trolley. Alternatively a backpack that you can carry comfortably on your back, or even a duffel bag that you can carry easily by hand or sling across your body are also great options. Whatever you choose, one thing to keep in mind is that the luggage itself should not weigh a ton, this will give you the flexibility to bring along one extra pair of shoes if you so desire.

>TOURIST

2. CARRY THE MINIMUM NUMBER OF BAGS

Selecting light weight luggage is not everything. You need to restrict the number of bags you carry as well. One carry-on size bag is ideal for light travel. Most carriers allow one cabin baggage plus one purse, handbag or camera bag as long as it slides under the seat in front. So technically, you can carry two items of luggage without checking them in.

3. PACK ONE EXTRA BAG

Always pack one extra empty bag along with your essential items. This could be a very light weight duffel bag or even a sturdy tote bag which takes up minimal space. In the event that you end up buying a lot of souvenirs, you already have a handy bag to stuff all that into and do not have to spend time hunting for an appropriate bag.

I'm very strict with my packing and have everything in its right place. I never change a rule. I hardly use anything in the hotel room. I wheel my own wardrobe in and that's it.

Charlie Watts

CLOTHES & ACCESSORIES

4. PLAN AHEAD

Figure out in advance what you plan to do on your trip. That will help you to pick that one dress you need for the occasion. If you are going to attend a wedding then you have to carry formal wear. If not, you can ditch the gown for something lighter that will be comfortable during long walks or on the beach.

5. WEAR THAT JACKET

Remember that wearing items will not add extra luggage for your air travel. So wear that bulky jacket that you plan to carry for your trip. This saves space and can also help keep you warm during the chilly flight.

6. MIX AND MATCH

Carry clothes that can be interchangeably used to reinvent your look. Find one top that goes well with a couple of pairs of pants or skirts. Use tops, shirts and jackets wisely along with other accessories like a scarf or a stole to create a new look.

7. CHOOSE YOUR FABRIC WISELY

Stuffing clothes in cramped bags definitely takes its toll which results in wrinkles. It is best to carry wrinkle free, synthetic clothes or merino tops. This will eliminate the need for that small iron you usually bring along.

8. DITCH CLOTHES PACK UNDERWEAR

Pack more underwear and socks. These are the things that will give you a fresh feel even if you do not get a chance to wear fresh clothes. Moreover these are easy to wash and can be dried inside the hotel room itself.

9. CHOOSE DARK OVER LIGHT

While picking your clothes choose dark coloured ones. They are easy to colour coordinate and can last longer before needing a wash. Accidental food spills and dirt from the road are less visible on darker clothes.

10. WEAR YOUR JEANS

Take only one pair of Jeans with you, which you should wear on the flight. Remember to pick a pair that can be worn for sightseeing trips and is equally eloquent for dinner. You can add variety by adding light weight cargoes and chinos.

11. CARRY SMART ACCESSORIES

The right accessory can give you a fresh look even with the same old dress. An intelligent neck-piece, a couple of bright scarves, stoles or a sarong can be used in a number of ways to add variety to your clothing. These light weight beauties can double up as a nursing cover, a light blanket, beach wear, a modesty cover for visiting places of worship, and also makes for an enthralling game of peek-a-boo.

12. LEARN TO FOLD YOUR GARMENTS

Seasoned travellers all swear by rolling their clothes for compact and wrinkle free packing. Bundle packing, where you roll the clothes around a central object as if tying it up, is also a popular method of compact and wrinkle free packing. Stacking folded clothes one on top of another is a big no-no as it makes creases extreme and they are difficult to get rid of without ironing.

13. WASH YOUR DIRTY LAUNDRY

One of the ways to avoid carrying loads of clothes is to wash the clothes you carry. At some places you might get to use the laundry services or a Laundromat but if you are in a pinch, best solution is to wash them yourself. If that is the plan then carrying quick drying clothes is highly recommended, which most often also happen to be the wrinkle free variety.

14. LEAVE THOSE TOWELS BEHIND

Regular towels take up a lot of space, are heavy and take ages to dry out. If you are staying at hotels they will provide you with towels anyway. If you are travelling to a remote place, where the availability of towels look doubtful, carry a light weight travel towel of viscose material to do the job.

15. USE A COMPRESSION BAG

Compression bags are getting lots of recommendation now days from regular travellers. These are useful for saving space in your luggage when you have to pack bulky dresses. While packing for the return trip, get help from the hotel staff to arrange a vacuum cleaner.

FOOTWEAR

16. PUT ON YOUR HIKING BOOTS

If you have plans to go hiking or trekking during your trip, you will need those bulky hiking boots. The best way to carry them is to wear them on flight to save space and luggage weight. You can remove the boots once inside and be comfortable in your socks.

17. PICKING THE RIGHT SHOES

Shoes are often the bulkiest items, along with being the dainty if you are a female. They need care and take up a lot of space in your luggage. It is advisable therefore to pick shoes very carefully. If you plan to do a lot of walking and site seeing, then wearing a pair of comfortable walking shoes are a must. For more formal occasions you can carry durable, light weight flats which will not take up much space.

18. STUFF SHOES

If you happen to pack a pair of shoes, ensure you utilize their hollow insides. Tuck small items like rolled up socks or belts to save space. They will also be easy to find.

\>TOURIST

TOILETRIES

19. STASHING TOILETRIES

Carry only absolute necessities. Airline rules dictate that for one carry-on bag, liquids and gels must be in 3.4 ounce (100ml) bottles or less, and must be packed in a one quart zip-lock bag. If you are planning to stay in a hotel, the basic things will be provided for you. It's best is to buy the rest from the local market at your destination.

20. TAKE ALONG TAMPONS

Tampons are a hard to find item in a lot of countries. Figure out how many you need and pack accordingly. For longer stays you can buy them online and have them delivered to where you are staying.

21. GET PAMPERED BEFORE YOU TRAVEL

Some avid travellers suggest getting a pedicure and manicure just the day before travelling. This not only gives you a well kept look, you also save the trouble of packing nail polish. Remember, every little bit of weight reduced adds up.

ELECTRONICS

22. LUGGING ALONG ELECTRONICS

Electronics have a large role to play in our lives today. Most of us cannot imagine our lives away from our phones, laptops or tablets. However while travelling, one must consider the amount of weight these electronics add to our luggage. Thankfully smart phones come along with all the essentials tools like a camera, email access, picture editing tools and more. They are smart to the point of eliminating the need to carry multiple gadgets. Choose a smart phone that suits all your requirements and travel with the world in your palms or pocket.

23. REDUCE THE NUMBER OF CHARGERS

If you do travel with multiple electronic devices, you will have to bear the additional burden of carrying all their chargers too. Check if a single charger can be used for multiple devices. You might also consider investing in a pocket charger. These small devices support multiple devices while keeping you charged on the go.

>TOURIST

24. TRAVEL FRIENDLY APPS

Along with smart phones come numerous apps, which are immensely helpful in our travels. You name it and you have an app for it at hand – take pictures, sharing with friends and family, torch to light dark roads, maps, checking flight/train times, find hotels and many other things. Use these smart alternatives to traditional items like books to eliminate weight and save space.

> *I get ideas about what's essential when packing my suitcase.*

-Diane von Furstenberg

TRAVELLING WITH KIDS

25. BRING ALONG THE STROLLER

Kids might enjoy walking for a while but they soon tire out and a stroller is the just the right thing for them to rest in while you continue your tour. Strollers also double duty as a luggage carrier and shopping bag holder. Remember to pick a light weight, easy to handle brand of stroller. Better yet, find out in advance if you can rent a stroller at your destination.

26. BRING ONLY ENOUGH DIAPERS FOR YOUR TRIP

Diapers take up a lot of space and add to the weight of your luggage. Therefore it is advisable to carry just enough diapers to last through the trip and a few for afterwards, till you buy fresh stock at your destination. Unless of course you are travelling to a really remote area, in which case you have no choice but to carry the load. Otherwise diapers are something you will find pretty easily.

27. TAKE ONLY A COUPLE OF TOYS

Children are easily attracted by new things in their environment. While travelling they will find numerous 'new' objects to scrutinize and play with. Packing just one favorite toy is enough, or if there is no favorite toy leave out all of them in favor of stories or imaginary games.

28. CARRY KID FRIENDLY SNACKS

Create a small snack counter in your bag to store away quick bites for those sudden hunger pangs. Depending on the child's age this could include chocolates, raisins, dry fruits, granola bars or biscuits. Also keep a bottle of water handy for your little one.

>TOURIST

These things do not add much weight and can be adjusted in a handbag or knapsack.

29. GAMES TO CARRY

Create some travel specific, imaginary games if you have slightly grown up children, like spot the attractions. Keep a coloring book and colors handy for in-flight or hotel time. Apps on your smart phone can keep the children engaged with cartoons and story books. Older children are often entertained by games available on phones or tablets. This cuts the weight of luggage down while keeping the kids entertained.

30. LET THE KIDS CARRY THEIR LOAD

A good thing is to start early sharing of responsibilities. Let your child pick a bag of his or her choice and pack it themselves. Keep tabs on what they are stuffing in their bags by asking if they will be using that item on the trip. It could start out being just an entertainment bag initially but with growing years they will learn to sort the useful from the superfluous. Children as little as four can maneuver a small trolley suitcase like a pro- their experience in pull along toys credit. If you are worried that you may be pulling it for them, you may want to start with a backpack.

31. DECIDE ON LOCATION FOR CHILDREN TO SLEEP

While on a trip you might not always get a crib at your destination, and carrying one will make life all the more difficult. Instead call ahead to see if there are any cribs or roll out beds for children. You may even put blankets on the floor. Weave them a story about camping and they will gladly sleep without any trouble.

32. GET BABY PRODUCTS DELIVERED AT YOUR DESTINATION

If you are absolutely paranoid about not getting your favourite variety of diaper or brand of baby food, check out online stores like amazon.com for services in your destination city. You can buy things online ahead of your travel and get them delivered to your hotel upon arrival.

33. FEEDING NEEDS OF YOUR INFANTS

If you are travelling with a breastfed infant, you save the trouble of carrying bottles and bottle sanitization kits. For special food, or medications, you may need

>TOURIST

to call ahead to make sure you have a refrigerator where you are staying.

34. FEEDING NEEDS OF YOUR TODDLER

With the progression from infancy to toddler, their dietary requirements too evolve. You will have to pack some snacks for travelling time. Fresh fruits and vegetables can be purchased at your destination. Most of the cities you travel to in whichever part of the world, will have baby food products and formulas, available at the local drug-store or the supermarket.

35. PICKING CLOTHES FOR YOUR BABY

Contrary to popular belief, babies can do without many changes of clothes. At the most pack 2 outfits per day. Pack mix and match type clothes for your little one as well. Pick things which are comfortable to wear and quick to dry.

36. SELECTING SHOES FOR YOUR BABY

Like outfits, kids can make do with two pairs of comfortable shoes. If you can get some water resistant shoes it will be best. To expedite drying wet shoes, you can stuff newspaper in them then wrap them with newspaper and leave them to dry overnight.

37. KEEP ONE CHANGE OF CLOTHES HANDY

Travelling with kids can be tricky. Keep a change of clothes for the kids and mum handy in your purse or tote bag. This takes a bit of space in your hand luggage but comes extremely handy in case there are any accidents or spills.

38. LEAVE BEHIND BABY ACCESSORIES

Baby accessories like their bed, bath tub, car seat, crib etc. should be left at home. Many hotels provide a crib on request, while car seats can be borrowed from friends or rented. Babies can be given a bath in the hotel sink or even in the adult bath tub with a little bit of water. If you bring a few bath toys, they can be used in the bath, pool, and out of water. They can also be sanitized easily in the sink.

39. CARRY A SMALL LOAD OF PLASTIC BAGS

With children around there are chances of a number of soiled clothes and diapers. These plastic bags help to sort the dirt from the clean inside your big bag.

>TOURIST

These are very light weight and come in handy to other carry stuff as well at times.

PACK WITH A PURPOSE

40. PACKING FOR BUSINESS TRIPS

One neutral-colored suit should suffice. It can be paired with different shirts, ties and accessories for different occasions. One pair of black suit pants could be worn with a matching jacket for the office or with a snazzy top for dinner.

41. PACKING FOR A CRUISE

Most cruises have formal dinners, and that formal dress usually takes up a lot of space. However you might find a tuxedo to rent. For women, a short black dress with multiple accessory options will do the trick.

42. PACKING FOR A LONG TRIP OVER DIFFERENT CLIMATES

The secret packing mantra for travel over multiple climates is layering. Layering traps air around your body creating insulation against the cold. The same light t-shirt that is comfortable in a warmer climate can be the innermost layer in a colder climate.

REDUCE SOME MORE WEIGHT

43. LEAVE PRECIOUS THINGS AT HOME

Things that you would hate to lose or get damaged leave them at home. Precious jewelry, expensive gadgets or dresses, could be anything. You will not require these on your trip. Leave them at home and spare the load on your mind.

44. SEND SOUVENIRS BY MAIL

If you have spent all your money on purchasing souvenirs, carrying them back in the same bag that you brought along would be difficult. Either pack everything in another bag and check it in the airport or get everything shipped to your home. Use an international carrier for a secure transit, but this could be more expensive than the checking fees at the airport.

45. AVOID CARRYING BOOKS

Books equal to weight. There are many reading apps which you can download on your smart phone or tab.

>TOURIST

Plus there are gadgets like Kindle and Nook that are thinner and lighter alternatives to your regular book.

CHECK, GET, SET, CHECK AGAIN

46. STRATEGIZE BEFORE PACKING

Create a travel list and prepare all that you think you need to carry along. Keep everything on your bed or floor before packing and then think through once again – do I really need that? Any item that meets this question can be avoided. Remove whatever you don't really need and pack the rest.

47. TEST YOUR LUGGAGE

Once you have fully packed for the trip take a test trip with your luggage. Take your bags and go to town for window shopping for an hour. If you enjoy your hour long trip it is good to go, if not, go home and reduce the load some more. Repeat this test till you hit the right weight.

48. ADD A ROLL OF DUCT TAPE

You might wonder why, when this book has been talking about reducing stuff, we're suddenly asking you to pack something totally unusual. This is because when you have limited supplies, duct tape is immensely helpful for small repairs – a broken bag, leaking zip-lock bag, broken sunglasses, you name it and duct tape can fix it, temporarily.

49. LIST OF ESSENTIAL ITEMS

Even though the emphasis is on packing light, there are things which have to be carried for any trip. Here is our list of essentials:

- Passport/Visa or any other ID

- Any other paper work that might be required on a trip like permits, hotel reservation confirmations etc.

- Medicines – all your prescription medicines and emergency kit, especially if you are travelling with children

- Medical or vaccination records

- Money in foreign currency if travelling to a different country

- Tickets- Email or Message them to your phone

>TOURIST

50. MAKE THE MOST OF YOUR TRIP

Wherever you are going, whatever you hope to do we encourage you to embrace it whole-heartedly. Take in the scenery, the culture and above all, enjoy your time away from home.

On a long journey even a straw weighs heavy.

-Spanish Proverb

>TOURIST

PACKING AND PLANNING TIPS

A Week before Leaving

- Arrange for someone to take care of pets and water plants.
- Stop mail and newspaper.
- Notify Credit Card companies where you are going.
- Change your thermostat settings.
- Car inspected, oil is changed, and tires have the correct pressure.
- Passports and photo identification is up to date.
- Pay bills.
- Copy important items and download travel Apps.
- Start collecting small bills for tips.

Right Before Leaving

- Clean out refrigerator.
- Empty garbage cans.
- Lock windows.
- Make sure you have the proper identification with you.
- Bring cash for tips.
- Remember travel documents.
- Lock door behind you.
- Remember wallet.
- Unplug items in house and pack chargers.

>TOURIST

READ OTHER GREATER THAN A TOURIST BOOKS

Greater Than a Tourist San Miguel de Allende Guanajuato Mexico: 50 Travel Tips from a Local by Tom Peterson

Greater Than a Tourist – Lake George Area New York USA: 50 Travel Tips from a Local by Janine Hirschklau

Greater Than a Tourist – Monterey California United States: 50 Travel Tips from a Local by Katie Begley

Greater Than a Tourist – Chanai Crete Greece: 50 Travel Tips from a Local by Dimitra Papagrigoraki

Greater Than a Tourist – The Garden Route Western Cape Province South Africa: 50 Travel Tips from a Local by Li-Anne McGregor van Aardt

Greater Than a Tourist – Sevilla Andalusia Spain: 50 Travel Tips from a Local by Gabi Gazon

Greater Than a Tourist – Kota Bharu Kelantan Malaysia: 50 Travel Tips from a Local by Aditi Shukla

Children's Book: Charlie the Cavalier Travels the World by Lisa Rusczyk

>TOURIST

> TOURIST

Visit Greater Than a Tourist for Free Travel Tips
http://GreaterThanATourist.com

Sign up for the Greater Than a Tourist Newsletter for discount days, new books, and travel information:
http://eepurl.com/cxspyf

Follow us on Facebook for tips, images, and ideas:
https://www.facebook.com/GreaterThanATourist

Follow us on Pinterest for travel tips and ideas:
http://pinterest.com/GreaterThanATourist

Follow us on Instagram for beautiful travel images:
http://Instagram.com/GreaterThanATourist

>TOURIST

> TOURIST

At Greater Than a Tourist, we love to share travel tips with you. How did we do? What guidance do you have for how we can give you better advice for your next trip? Please send your feedback to GreaterThanaTourist@gmail.com as we continue to improve the series. We appreciate your constructive feedback. Thank you.

>TOURIST

METRIC CONVERSIONS

TEMPERATURE

110° F — — 40° C
100° F —
90° F — — 30° C
80° F —
70° F — — 20° C
60° F —
50° F — — 10° C
40° F —
32° F — — 0° C
20° F —
10° F — — -10° C
0° F — — -18° C
-10° F —
-20° F — — -30° C

To convert F to C:
Subtract 32, and then multiply by 5/9 or .5555.

To Convert C to F:
Multiply by 1.8 and then add 32.

32F = 0C

LIQUID VOLUME

To Convert:..................Multiply by
U.S. Gallons to Liters................. 3.8
U.S. Liters to Gallons .... .26
Imperial Gallons to U.S. Gallons 1.2
Imperial Gallons to Liters....... 4.55
Liters to Imperial Gallons .... .22
1 Liter = .26 U.S. Gallon
1 U.S. Gallon = 3.8 Liters

DISTANCE

To convert ....Multiply by
Inches to Centimeters 2.54
Centimeters to Inches .... .39
Feet to Meters....................... .3
Meters to Feet 3.28
Yards to Meters .... .91
Meters to Yards 1.09
Miles to Kilometers 1.61
Kilometers to Miles............ .62
1 Mile = 1.6 km
1 km = .62 Miles

WEIGHT

1 Ounce = .28 Grams
1 Pound = .4555 Kilograms
1 Gram = .04 Ounce
1 Kilogram = 2.2 Pounds

>TOURIST

TRAVEL QUESTIONS

- Do you bring presents home to family or friends after a vacation?
- Do you get motion sick?
- Do you have a favorite billboard?
- Do you know what to do if there is a flat tire?
- Do you like a sun roof open?
- Do you like to eat in the car?
- Do you like to wear sun glasses in the car?
- Do you like toppings on your ice cream?
- Do you use public bathrooms?
- Did you bring your cell phone and does it have power?
- Do you have a form of identification with you?
- Have you ever been pulled over by a cop?
- Have you ever given money to a stranger on a road trip?
- Have you ever taken a road trip with animals?
- Have you ever went on a vacation alone?
- Have you ever run out of gas?

- If you could move to any place in the world, where would it be?
- If you could travel anywhere in the world, where would you travel?
- If you could travel in any vehicle, which one would it be?
- If you had three things to wish for from a magic genie, what would they be?
- If you have a driver's license, how many times did it take you to pass the test?
- What are you the most afraid of on vacation?
- What do you want to get away from the most when you are on vacation?
- What foods smells bad to you?
- What item do you bring on ever trip with you away from home?
- What makes you sleepy?
- What song would you love to hear on the radio when you're cruising on the highway?
- What travel job would you want the least?
- What will you miss most while you are away from home?
- What is something you always wanted to try?

\>TOURIST

- What is the best road side attraction that you ever saw?
- What is the farthest distance you ever biked?
- What is the farthest distance you ever walked?
- What is the weirdest thing you needed to buy while on vacation?
- What is your favorite candy?
- What is your favorite color car?
- What is your favorite family vacation?
- What is your favorite food?
- What is your favorite gas station drink or food?
- What is your favorite license plate design?
- What is your favorite restaurant?
- What is your favorite smell?
- What is your favorite song?
- What is your favorite sound that nature makes?
- What is your favorite thing to bring home from a vacation?
- What is your favorite vacation with friends?
- What is your favorite way to relax?

- Where is the farthest place you ever traveled in a car?
- Where is the farthest place you ever went North, South, East and West?
- Where is your favorite place in the world?
- Who is your favorite singer?
- Who taught you how to drive?
- Who will you miss the most while you are away?
- Who if the first person you will contact when you get to your destination?
- Who brought you on your first vacation?
- Who likes to travel the most in your life?
- Would you rather be hot or cold?
- Would you rather drive above, below, or at the speed limited?
- Would you rather drive on a highway or a back road?
- Would you rather go on a train or a boat?
- Would you rather go to the beach or the woods?

>TOURIST

TRAVEL BUCKET LIST

1.

2.

3.

4.

5.

6.

7.

8.

9.

10.

>TOURIST

NOTES

Made in the USA
Las Vegas, NV
19 February 2024

85981053R00073